First published by Walker Books Ltd in
Bear's Birthday (1985), *Help!* (1985),
Jumping (1985), *Make a Face* (1985),
Shirley's Shops (1986) and *So Can I* (1985)

This edition published 1998
Reprinted 1998

Text © 1985, 1986 Allan Ahlberg
Illustrations © 1985, 1986 Colin McNaughton

This book has been typeset in ITC Garamond Light.

Printed in Hong Kong

British Library Cataloguing in Publication Data
A catalogue record for this book is
available from the British Library.

ISBN 0-7445-5485-3

WHAT'S IN THE SHOP?

Allan Ahlberg + Colin McNaughton

WALKER BOOKS
AND SUBSIDIARIES
LONDON • BOSTON • SYDNEY

PUSH AND PULL

pull and push

push

and pull

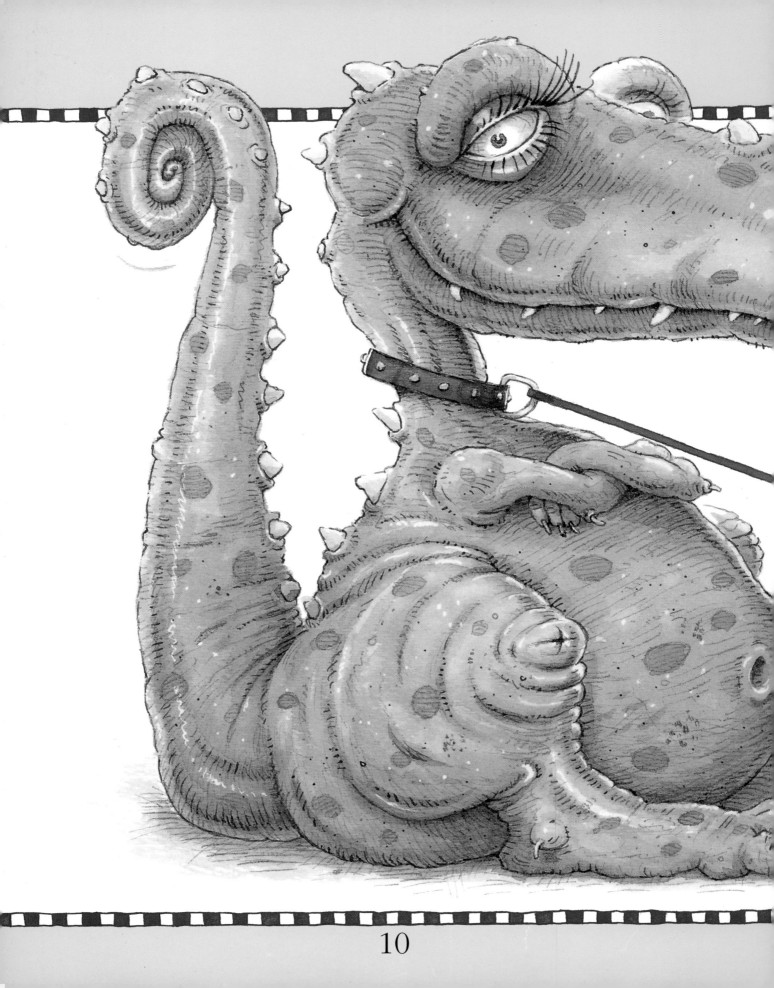

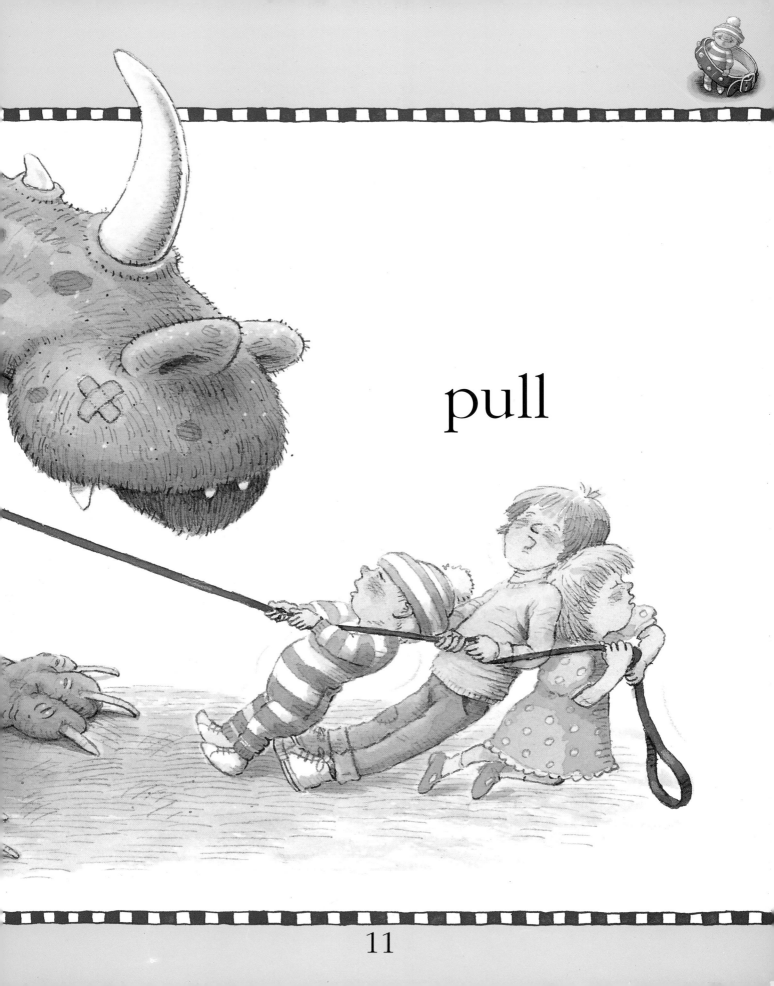

pull

and
push

CAR + CAR

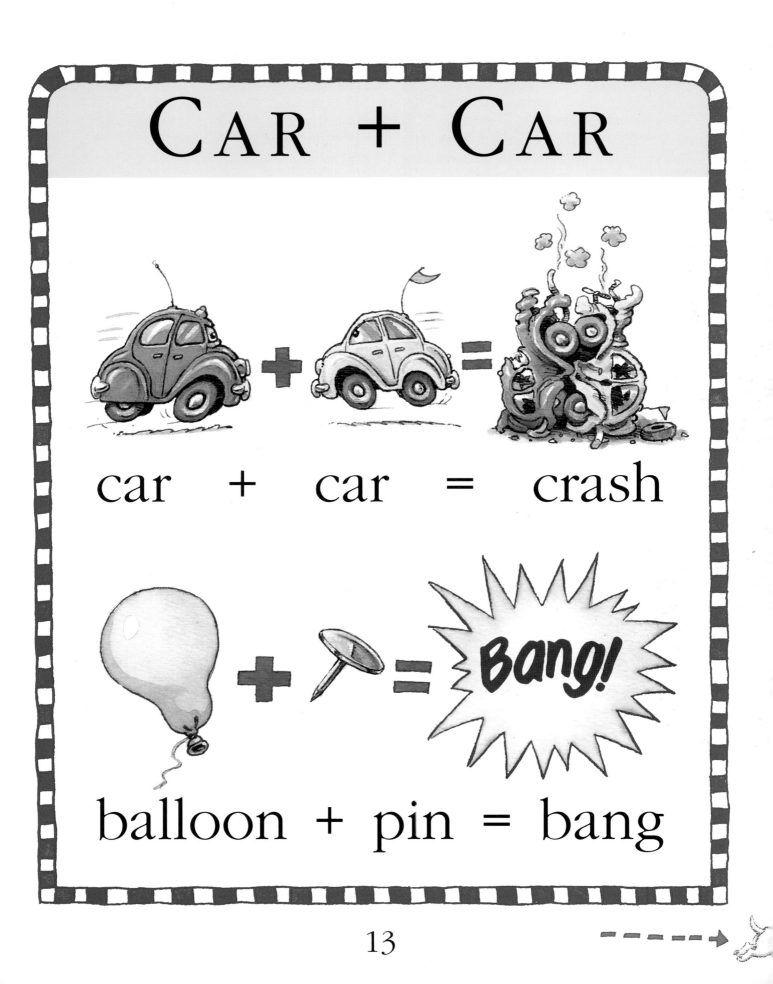

car + car = crash

balloon + pin = bang

elephant + water = squirt

I can brush my teeth.

So can I!

I can write my name.

Jumbo

So can I!

I can read a book.

I can carry the shopping.

So can I!

I can clean my teeth
and write my name
and read a book
and carry the shopping.

BIG HEAD

big head   little head   big ear   little ear

big eye   little eye   big nose   little nose

big mouth   little mouth

little hat…

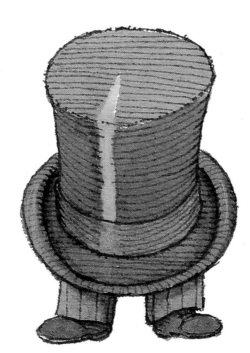

big hat

The shop is open.

In Shirley's sweet shop

there are:

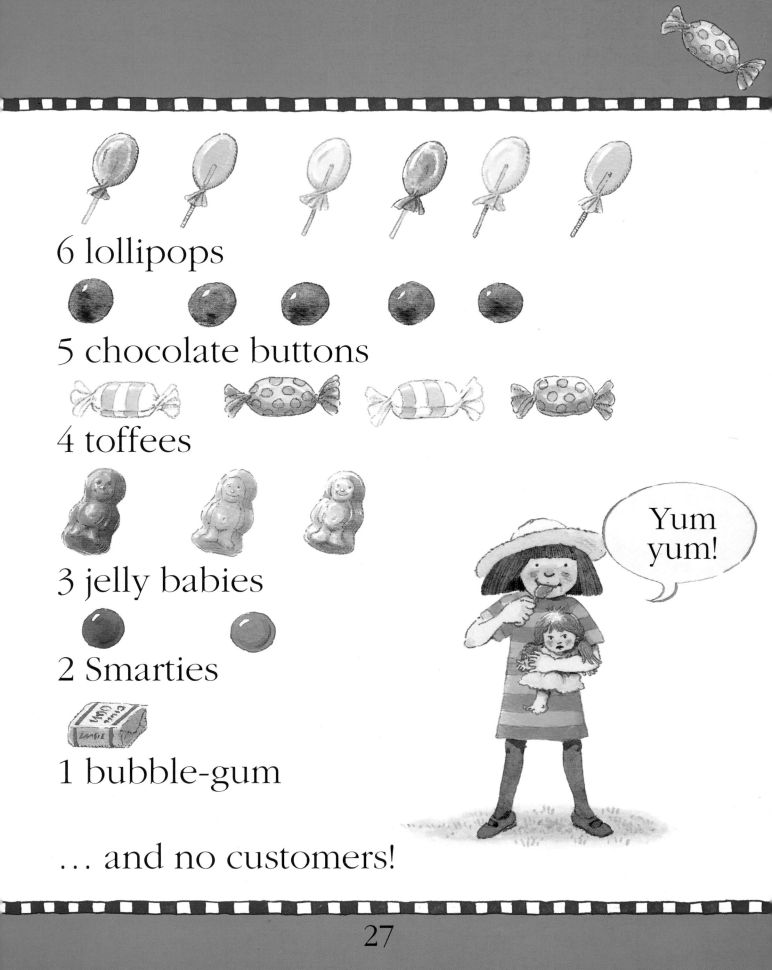

6 lollipops

5 chocolate buttons

4 toffees

3 jelly babies

2 Smarties

1 bubble-gum

... and no customers!

Yum yum!

In Shirley's dog shop
there are:

a big dog

a little dog

a very little dog

a round dog

a square dog

two spotty dogs ...

I'm off!

and a hot dog!

In Shirley's honey shop
there are pots of honey …

and lots of bees!

Buzz off!

In Shirley's weather shop
there are …

rain

fog

snow

wind

blue skies and sunny periods

In Shirley's tea shop
there are:

cups and plates

knives, forks and spoons

cakes and biscuits

crisps and sandwiches

fizzy drink ...

and a few friends.

BOY + BOY

boy + boy + boy + boy

+ boy + boy + boy + boy

+ boy + boy + boy + boy

+ boy + boy + boy =

a pile of boys

before the haircut

after the haircut

before the game

after the game

before the bath

after the bath

before bedtime...

...and after

the end

MORE WALKER PAPERBACKS
For You to Enjoy

Also by Allan Ahlberg and Colin McNaughton

PUT ON A SHOW!

You'll find creatures of all shapes and sizes – from worms to monsters,
from frogs to dogs – in this madcap menagerie of single words and phrases,
simple sentences and memorable rhymes from the popular Red Nose Reader series.

"The learning to read process has never been more enjoyable."
Books For Your Children

0-7445-4756-3   £5.99

WHO STOLE THE PIE?

You'll find food of all sorts – from pies to cakes to the most enormous sandwich ever –
in this hilarious hot-pot of single words and phrases, simple sentences and memorable rhymes
from the popular Red Nose Reader series.

"The kind of obvious but nutty humour that sends five-year-olds into fits of giggles."
The Guardian

0-7445-4757-1   £5.99

TELL US A STORY

Two little boys climbed up to bed. "Tell us a story, Dad," they said.
But one story leads to another – and another…

"Brilliantly done … very humorous … perfect for children of four to six."
Tony Bradman, Parents

0-7445-3614-6   £4.50